ChordTime® Piano

LEVEL 2B

中国乐曲

MUSIC FROM CHINA

Arranged by Nancy and Randall Faber

This book belongs to: _____

Topic Planning: Yishan Zhao
Production Coordinator: Jon Ophoff
Editor/Researcher: Patrick Bachmann
Translator/Editor: Lin Tian
Design and Illustration: Terpstra Design, Wagner Design
Engraving: Dovetree Productions, Inc.

978-1-61677-726-5

A NOTE TO TEACHERS

ChordTime® Piano Music from China
is a colorful, musical tour of China with
rhythmic dances, serene folk melodies, and
original Chinese piano works. The book is
arranged for the mid-elementary pianist
and loosely correlates with Level 2B in the
Piano Adventures method. In this collection:

- Melodies are in the keys of **C major**,
  G major, **A minor**, and **E minor**.
  Harmony is often built on intervals
  of the **2nd**, **4th**, **and 5th**, typical of
  Chinese music.

- Staccatos, accents, slurs, and use
  of the damper pedal add rhythmic
  vitality and **color**.

- The music is from **various provinces**
  throughout China.

- Original and arranged piano pieces
  by **Chinese composers** are featured.

- A **Duet Improvisation** and **Guided
  Student Composition** help students
  create their own "sounds of China."

Helpful Hints:

1. Hands-alone practice is often helpful
   to focus on fingering and melodic and
   rhythmic patterns. Assign challenging
   measures for special repetitive practice.

2. Pay close attention to balance. The
   melody should be played with a singing
   tone supported by a light accompaniment.

3. In Chinese music, it is especially
   important to observe all of the articulation
   marks including the slur, staccato, accent,
   and tenuto.

4. The student may go through several
   ChordTime books, which offer a
   variety of styles, before moving up to
   FunTime Piano (Level 3A-3B).

Hi, I'm **LeLe*** (pronounced Luh-Luh),
the musical panda from China.
Look for me in the book for
important music pointers!

C h o r d T i m e   P i a n o

* The Chinese character 乐 "Le" has two meanings,
one is music and the other is happy!

CONTENTS

A Picture Tour of China 4-5

The Sound of China 6-7
The C Pentatonic Scale
The A Minor Pentatonic Scale
Duet Improvisation Activity

Picking Flowers 8-9
Sichuan Folk Song
Arranged by Li Yinghai
LeLe's Performance Tip

The Little Bird Song 10-11
Composed by Li Chongguang
LeLe's Performance Tips

Divertimento (Zhi Mode) 12-13
Composed by Sang Tong
LeLe's Performance Tips

Talk Back 14-15
Hebei Folk Song
Arranged by Li Yinghai
LeLe's Performance Tips

Luchai Flowers 16-19
Jiangsu Folk Song
LeLe's Performance Tips
Duet Improvisation Activity

The Luhua Rooster 20-21
Composed by Ding Shande
LeLe's Performance Tips

Little Dance Song 22-23
Composed by Ding Shande
LeLe's Performance Tips

Lady Meng Jiang 24-27
Jiangsu Folk Song
Performance Tips

The Composer Is You! 28-29
Guided Student Composition

Dictionary Puzzle 30-31

Music Dictionary 32

A PICTURE TOUR OF CHINA

CITIES

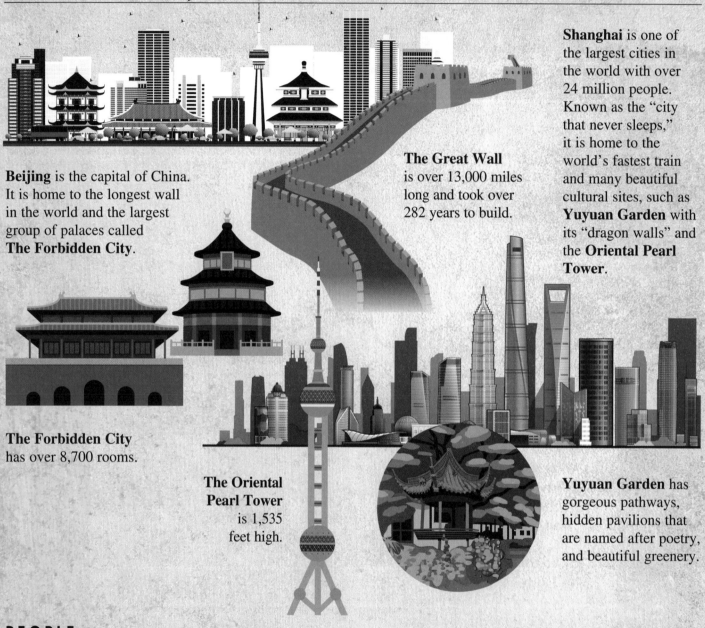

Beijing is the capital of China. It is home to the longest wall in the world and the largest group of palaces called **The Forbidden City**.

The Great Wall is over 13,000 miles long and took over 282 years to build.

Shanghai is one of the largest cities in the world with over 24 million people. Known as the "city that never sleeps," it is home to the world's fastest train and many beautiful cultural sites, such as **Yuyuan Garden** with its "dragon walls" and the **Oriental Pearl Tower**.

The Forbidden City has over 8,700 rooms.

The Oriental Pearl Tower is 1,535 feet high.

Yuyuan Garden has gorgeous pathways, hidden pavilions that are named after poetry, and beautiful greenery.

PEOPLE

Amazing **ice sculptors** in northeast China create fantastic shapes.

Representation of an **emperor** from Chinese history.

Folk dancers in northwest China are famous for their skilled dancing and singing.

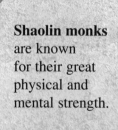

Shaolin monks are known for their great physical and mental strength.

SIGHTS

Elephant Trunk Hill
This rock formation looks like an elephant drinking water with its trunk from the Li River. Can you see it?

trunk→

elephant body↑

Detian Waterfall
A beautiful, famous waterfall between China and Vietnam.

Terracotta Army
This sculpted army was created by the Emperor over 2,000 years ago. Archeologists have discovered over 8,000 soldiers, 130 chariots, and 670 horses. More than 700,000 people worked on the Terracotta Army and each terracotta warrior is a unique figure. It is considered one of the great wonders of the world.

Huts of the Yurts
A portable, round tent used in Inner Mongolia that can have interesting designs.

ANIMALS

Tibetan Antelope
Known for their long horns, these antelope live in very harsh conditions in Tibet, Qinghai, and Xinjiang.

Panda
The giant pandas live in south central China and are considered a national treasure. Notice the large black patches around the eyes, ears, and around the body.

Wild Horses
Once extinct, these beautiful wild horses now live in northwest China where there is a breeding center—the largest in Asia to protect these magnificent animals.

FOOD

Hotpot
A Chinese cooking style where food is cooked in a broth at the table and often dipped in sauces.

Lychee Tea
Lychee is a sweet fruit in Asia. The tea has a sweet, honey taste.

Dim Sum
A meal of sweet and tasty small dishes, including buns, noodles, dumplings, cakes, rice and more.

Rice and Noodles
These are common dishes in China served with other main course items.

SOUNDS

Dombra
The dombra is a traditional instrument from west China. It has a long neck, two strings, and an oblong body. Its sound is sweet and unique.

THE SOUND OF CHINA

One of the unique sounds of Chinese music is the **pentatonic scale**.
In western music, the **major scale** is the most popular scale with 7 tones.

C Major Scale

1. Play the **C major scale** and listen to the sound.

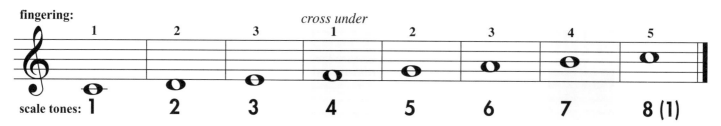

In Chinese music, the **4th** and **7th** tones are often not used.
This forms a 5-note scale called the **pentatonic scale**.
Penta means "five" and **tonic** means "tone." Think, five tones!

C Pentatonic Scale

2. Play the **C pentatonic scale** with all five fingers. Notice the *skip* between fingers **3** and **4**.
Are there any *half steps* in this scale? _____

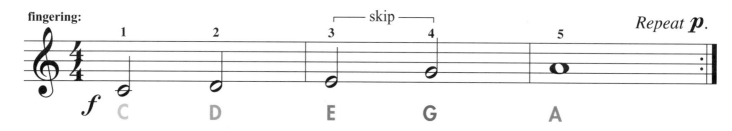

The first piece, "Picking Flowers" (**pp. 8-9**) uses the **A minor pentatonic scale**. This scale relates
to the **C pentatonic scale**. However, instead of *starting* and *ending* on C, it *starts* and *ends* on **A**.

Both scales share the **same letter names**!

A Minor Pentatonic Scale

3. Now play the **A minor pentatonic scale** with all five fingers. Notice the *skips*.
Are there any *half steps* in this scale? _____

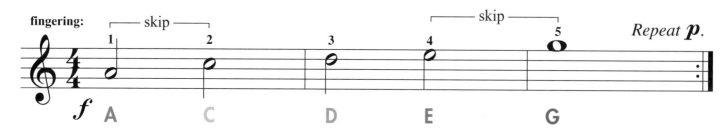

CREATING WITH THE A MINOR PENTATONIC SCALE

Here is the **A minor pentatonic scale** split between the left hand and right hand.

• Depress the **damper pedal** and play 5-6 times up and down until it's easy.

LeLe and a friend

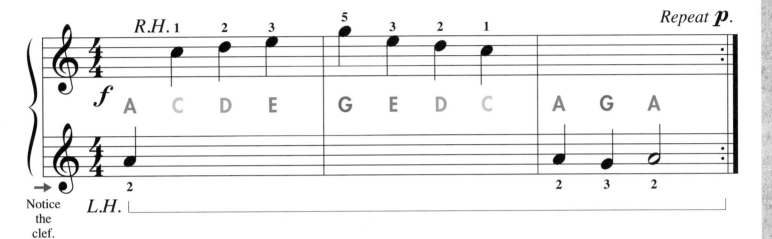

Notice the clef.

Duet Improvisation Activity

• Your teacher will play a duet based on "Picking Flowers" (**pp. 8-9**). Listen to the **tempo** and **mood**.

• When you are ready, create your *own* sounds with the **duet** using the **A minor pentatonic scale** shown above.

• Play the notes *in any order*. To **end**, the duet will s-l-o-w down and fade. You slow down, too! Imagine the footsteps in the garden slowly walking away.

Teacher Duet: (Student plays 1 octave HIGHER on the keyboard)

8

Introduction to *Picking Flowers*

Everyone enjoys picking flowers. This beautiful folk melody from Sichuan province has words that teach by describing what flowers can be picked during each month of the year. The lyrics help define the seasons, the vibrant growing time, and the wintertime—a quiet waiting for "frost-beaten plums that will open by themselves."

Translated lyrics:

In January, no flowers can be picked.

In February, the flowers begin to bloom.

In March, the peach blossom is like the sea.

In April, the vineyard opens.

In May, the pomegranates are tip to tip.

In June, the peonies.

In July, rice is made into wine.

In August, I smell the sweet fragrance of osmanthus flowers.

In September, embrace the chrysanthemums.

In October, the people love pine and cypress.

In December, during the winter, no flowers can be picked.

The frost-beaten plums will open by themselves.

LeLe's Performance Tip

- Imagine the L.H. staccato **A**'s in **m.*** **1** and **m. 3** are footsteps in the garden. Can you circle **4** other measures like this?

采花
Picking Flowers

Sichuan Folk Song
Arranged by Li Yinghai

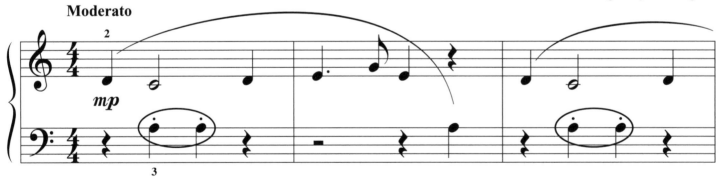

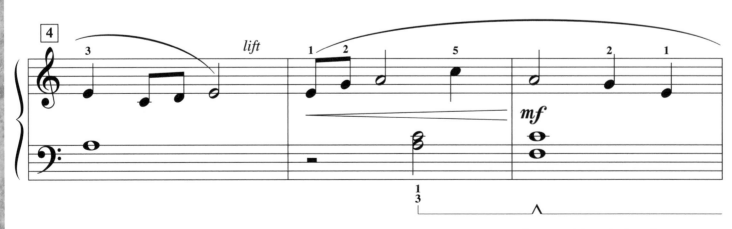

* **m.** – abbreviation for measure

9

LeLe's Performance Tips

"The Little Bird Song" imitates the sound of birds chirping in **mm.* 1-7.**

1. What **major** chord is used in **mm. 1-7**? (circle)

   G major   **C major**   **E major**

2. The opening **grace note** from **F♯** to **G** creates a "chirp."
   Is it a *half step* or *whole step*? _____

3. In **mm. 8-11**, is the harmony still **C major**? _____
   Circle the accompaniment pattern:

   waltz chord   Alberti bass   blocked chords

4. For **mm. 8-15**, imagine the **R.H. melody** is the bird in flight.
   Where does the harmony change to a **V7 chord**? **m.** _____

5. Where do the musical "chirps" return? **m.** _____
   At the end (**m. 21**), let your R.H. lift gracefully higher—as if
   the bird was flying to the top of a tree.

Tip: Accent the "chirp" and land *gently* on the note that follows.

小鸟之歌
The Little Bird Song

Allegretto

Composed by Li Chongguang

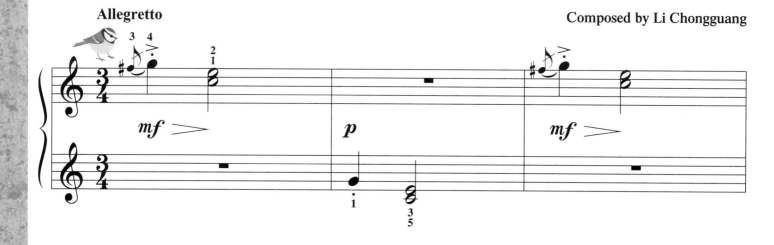

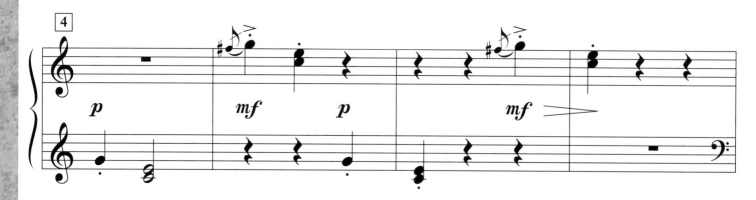

* **mm.** – measures (plural)

Tip: Accent the "chirp" and land gently.

The title of the next piece, "Divertimento," comes from the Italian word *divertire*, which means "to amuse." How might this piece musically amuse?

LeLe's Performance Tips

1. Have you ever looked at something upside down?
   The composer has amused us with this in **mm**. **1-2** and **mm**. **5-6**.
   Hint: Try it out, keeping the *staccatos* crisp and rhythmic.

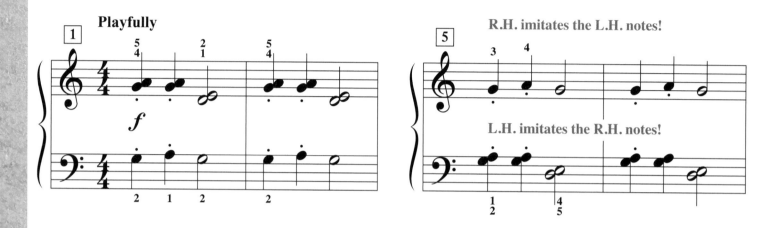

2. The **bold** start in **m. 1** is immediately followed by a *soft*, whimsical passage in **mm. 3-4**.
   Notice the fleeting L.H. 8th notes at **m. 3**. **Hint:** Keep your fingers close to the keys.

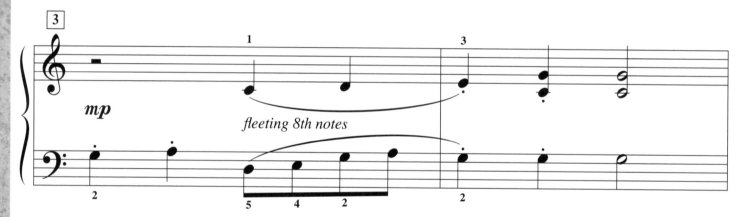

3. The same mischievous contrast continues for **mm. 5-8**.
   Can you spot this in the music? (See p. 13)

4. Now look at the **ending**.
   At **m. 9**, a *forte* chord is struck.
   The pedal sustains the sound
   as both hands plunge into the
   bass clef at **m. 10**.

   The *rit.* gives added drama,
   as if to say, "Game over!"

   Try this fun, theatrical ending!

This piece is built on the **C pentatonic scale**.

C   D   E   G   A

- What is **LeLe** showing us in the music?

嬉游曲（徵调式）
Divertimento (Zhi Mode)

Playfully

Composed by Sang Tong

cross 2 over
(1)

rit.

Introduction to *Talk Back* (p. 15)

This piece was originally written as a **duet** for two traditional **Chinese bamboo flutes**.
The bamboo wood produces a pleasing, mellow tone.

LeLe's Performance Tips

1. Let's imagine this duet as a *conversation* between two players.
   Which hand has the melody in **mm. 1-4**?   **R.H.** or **L.H.** (circle)

   Is the melody *staccato* or *legato*? _____

   Is the player speaking loudly or rather softly? _____

2. Which hand has the melody in **mm. 5-8**? **R.H.** or **L.H.** (circle)

   Is the melody *staccato* or *legato*? _____

3. Circle **3 things** that help make this
   an interesting conversation.

   – Contrasting articulation

   – A key change

   – A different octave range
     for each melodic "voice"

   – A tempo change to end
     the conversation

   – Many accidentals

4. This piece is built on **E** as the "home note" (*tonic*). However, its scale is related to the
   G pentatonic scale. Instead of *starting* and *ending* on **G**, it *starts* and *ends* on **E**.

   Play both scales several times until it's easy. Follow the **fingering** and notice where the *skips* occur.

   Do both scales share the **same letter names**? _____   Are there any *half steps* in either scale? _____

G Pentatonic Scale

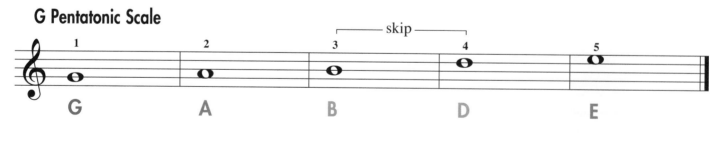

E Minor Pentatonic Scale

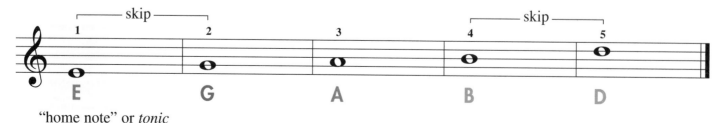

"home note" or *tonic*

顶嘴
Talk Back

Hebei Folk Song
Arranged by Li Yinghai

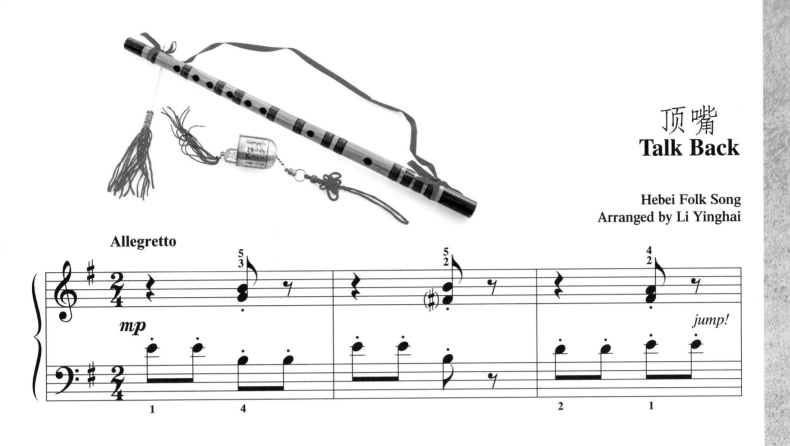

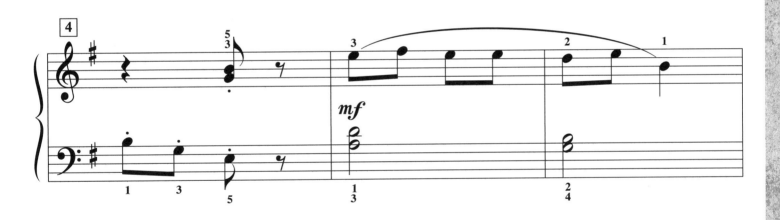

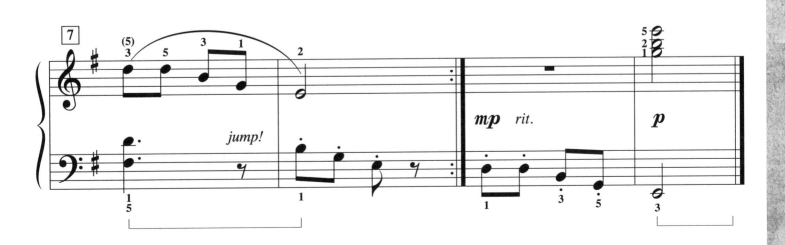

Introduction to *Luchai Flowers* (pp. 18-19)

The Luchai flower, common in Jiangsu province, is a reed flower that grows in the low wetlands and shallow water. Each year it blooms beautifully. The Luchai flower also symbolizes love.

The melody to this piece belongs to a category of folk songs known as "work songs." These types of melodies were improvised while people worked in the fields as a creative way to pass the time and make work seem less strenuous.

LeLe's Performance Tips (pp. 18-19)

1. When we do strenuous physical work, we need to take short breaks to *pause*, *rest*, and then *return* to the task. This piece captures this well with the use of **fermatas**.

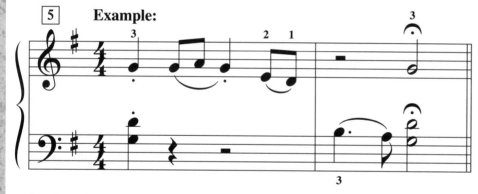

Can you find the *four* **fermatas** in the piece?

Mm. ___, ___, ___, and ___.

Hint: As you play, think of each fermata as a "little rest" to prepare for what's next!

2. Now imagine the working person becoming tired, s-l-o-w-i-n-g down (*rit.*), and perhaps loudly calling out, "Break time!"

   What two measures might fit this description? **Mm.** ____ and _____

3. At the end is an *accelerando e crescendo*. What do you think could be happening?
   Hint: Use **m**. 21 to prepare the L.H. shift for a confident ending!

accelerando e crescendo

f

prepare L.H.

CREATING WITH THE
G PENTATONIC SCALE

"Luchai Flowers" uses the **G pentatonic scale** split between the L.H. and R.H.

Follow the **fingering** and notice where the *skips* occur. Play several times until it's easy!

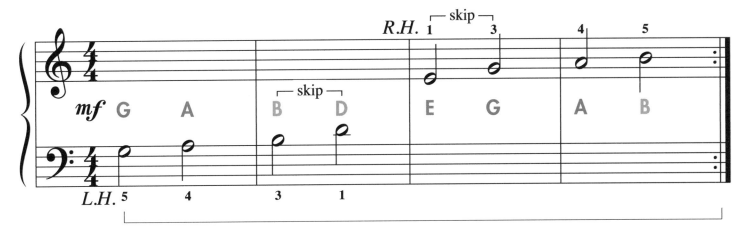

Duet Improvisation Activity

- Your teacher will play a duet based on the cheerful mood of "Luchai Flowers" (**pp. 18-19**).

- When you are ready, create your own sounds using the **G pentatonic scale** above.
  Play the notes *in any order*.

- When you hear a **trill*** in the teacher part, *slow down* and *pause*.
  Restart when your teacher begins again!

- To **end**, your teacher may cue you by whispering, "Luchai." End with a *forte* **G**!

Teacher Duet: (Student plays *as written*)

* trill – a rapid alternation of two keys next to each other.

• As you play this piece, bring out the **accents** and keep the *staccatos* crisp!

拔根芦柴花
Luchai Flowers

Jiangsu Folk Song

Cheerfully

Introduction to
The Luhua Rooster (p. 21)

The rooster is the tenth sign of the Chinese zodiac. An interesting fact is that 2017 was the last year of the rooster with the next one being in 2029. The symbolic meaning of the rooster in Chinese culture is that of honesty and punctuality (being on time). In ancient times, with no alarm clocks, the rooster was the timekeeper in signaling the official start of the day.

The rooster also symbolized the sun, as if the rooster and sun were partners together in bringing us the light of dawn.

With their bright red comb, colorful feathers, and golden tail, the rooster was considered beautiful and came to symbolize good luck. This piece by Ding Shande is from a collection titled "Happy Festival."

LeLe's Performance Tips

1.   **Mm. 1-8** of this piece are marked *forte*.
Imagine the melody of **mm. 1-4** as the confident crow of the rooster at dawn.

2. Play the melody *forte* phrasing off at the end of each "rooster call."
You and your teacher may have fun singing the **words**. Or enjoy singing on the syllable "**La.**"

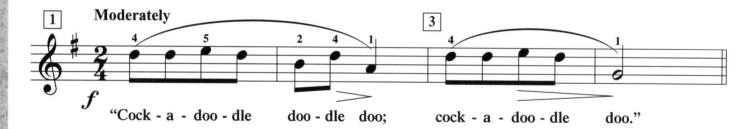

3. At **m. 9**, the character and texture change dramatically.
Check *four* ways the composer creates **contrast**.

_____ Use of *staccatos*   _____ Use of pedal

_____ Changing time signature   _____ Sudden L.H. activity

_____ Change of dynamics   _____ Use of accidentals

- Notice the L.H. fingering in **mm. 1-2** helps to keep a smooth *legato* from the **D** to **E**.

芦花公鸡
The Luhua Rooster

Composed by Ding Shande

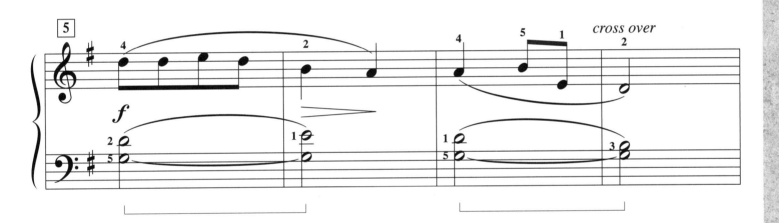

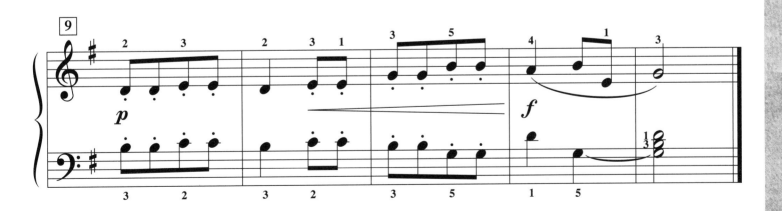

Introduction to *Little Dance Song* (p. 23)

"Little Dance Song," composed by Ding Shande, is the second piece in his collection called *Happy Festival*. It also uses the **G pentatonic scale**, like "The Luhua Rooster." Perhaps we could use our imagination and link these two pieces together. Let's suppose:

- After the rooster crows in "The Luhua Rooster," the chicks begin to stir as if starting a little dance.

- Or, after the rooster crows, a young person arrives and playfully tosses seeds around.

- Try performing the pieces "The Luhua Rooster" and "Little Dance Song" one after another. Then repeat "The Luhua Rooster" as a fun ending!

LeLe's Performance Tips

1. If you like playing **4ths**, you will enjoy playing this piece!
   Notice the L.H. **parallel 4ths**, which give a characteristic Chinese sound.
   Hint: Play the first 4th *staccato* and the second with a slight stress for the *tenuto mark*.

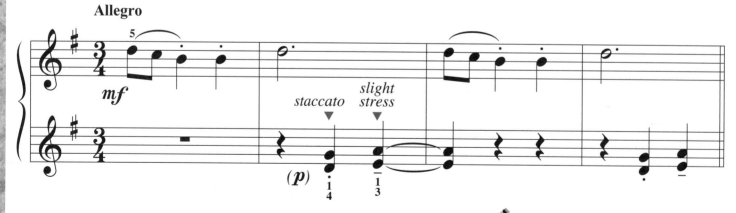

2. In what measure does the **L.H.** begin playing the melody? **m.** ____
   Is the melody the *same* as the **R.H.**? _____

3. Is the **L.H.** melody also the same *dynamic mark* as the opening **R.H.** melody? ____
   Hint: Bring out the *mf* with a warm tone to establish the new "soloist."

- Notice the piece begins with both hands playing in the **treble clef**.

- At **m. 6**, what does **LeLe** point out?

小舞曲
Little Dance Song

Composed by Ding Shande

Introduction to
Lady Meng Jiang (p. 26-27)

Lady Meng Jiang is a famous Chinese folktale. It tells the story of a woman whose husband is sent away for many years to work on the construction of the Great Wall. This song tells of her sadness throughout the different seasons of the year as she thinks of her husband.

This story is considered one of the "Four Great Chinese Love Folktales," the other three being: "Butterfly Lovers," "Legend of the White Snake," and "The Cowherd and the Weaver Girl."

Performance Tips

This piece uses the **C pentatonic scale** - C D E G A. However, instead of *starting* and *ending* on C, this scale *starts* and *ends* on **G**. For this reason, we can say it is the **C pentatonic scale starting on G**.

• Play each scale until it's easy. Follow the **fingering** and notice where the *skips* occur.

C Pentatonic Scale

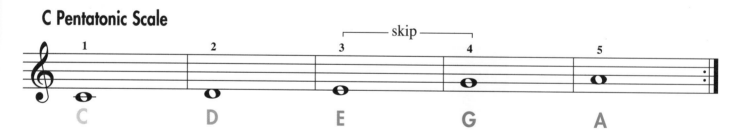

C Pentatonic Scale, starting on G

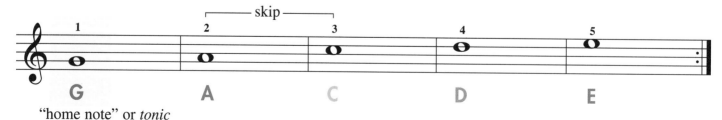

"home note" or *tonic*

Translated lyrics:

In spring, the flowers bloom,
Butterflies fly over the pink wall.

Although they are thousands of miles apart,
Meng Jiang meets her husband Wanqi Liang.

In summer, the wind blows,
Meng Jiang wanders in the garden.

Lotus flowers are in pairs,
This loving couple has to fly apart.

In fall, the plants are withered,
Yellow leaves are falling.

Birds can still come back to their nests,
Meng Jiang is floating like falling leaves.

In winter, snowflakes fly,
Meng Jiang sends clothes from thousands of miles away.

All kinds of hardships on the way,
This couple has to say goodbye forever.

This artistic piece has many expressive markings.

- Spot the following:
  mezzo-forte, *forte*, *pianissimo*, *diminuendo*, *ritardando*, *crescendo*, *accent*

孟姜女
Lady Meng Jiang

Jiangsu Folk Song

INTRO

Slowly, with majesty

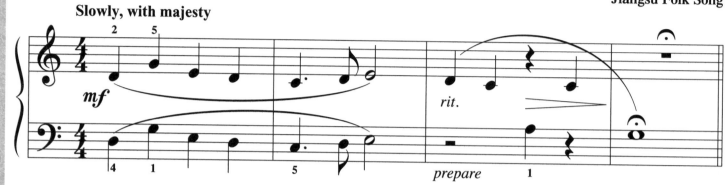

THEME

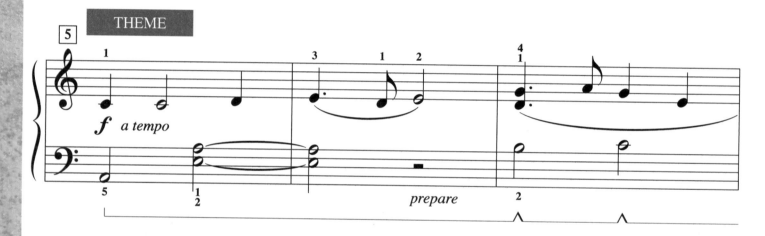

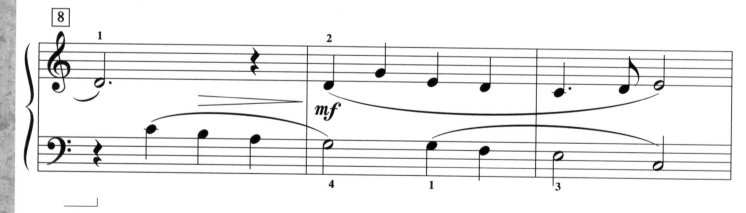

The Composer Is You!

In Chinese music, the **interval of a 4th** plays a prominent role in melodies and harmonies.

Remember, an interval is the *distance between 2 notes* on the keyboard or staff.
A **4th** spans four letter names. (Ex. D - G)

In "Talk Back" (**p. 23**), each hand played **4ths** for the "harmonic background."

You can compose your *own* piece by:

- Using *only* **R.H. blocked 4ths**. Choose from the **4ths** below.

- Depress the **damper pedal** and explore playing the **4ths** *in any order*.

- When you are ready, add the **L.H. 5ths** (**p. 29**). Use the **sample rhythm** given or create your own. After exploring several possibilities, write down your favorite!

Composition Toolbox of 4ths

Choose finger combinations of **1-3**, **1-4**, or **2-5** to best fit your hand movement.

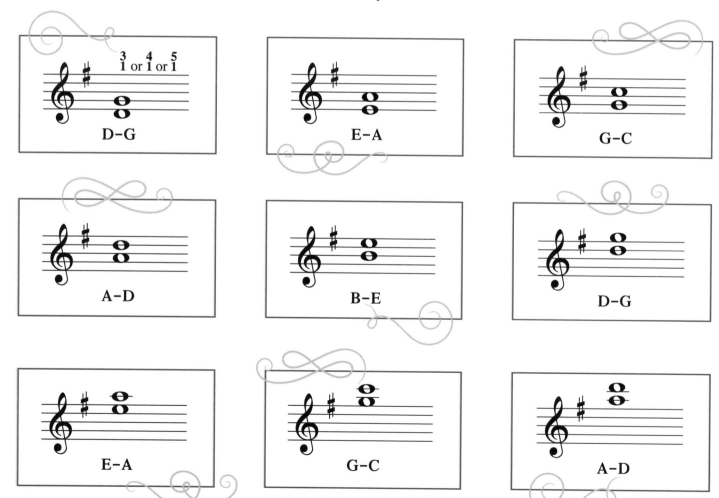

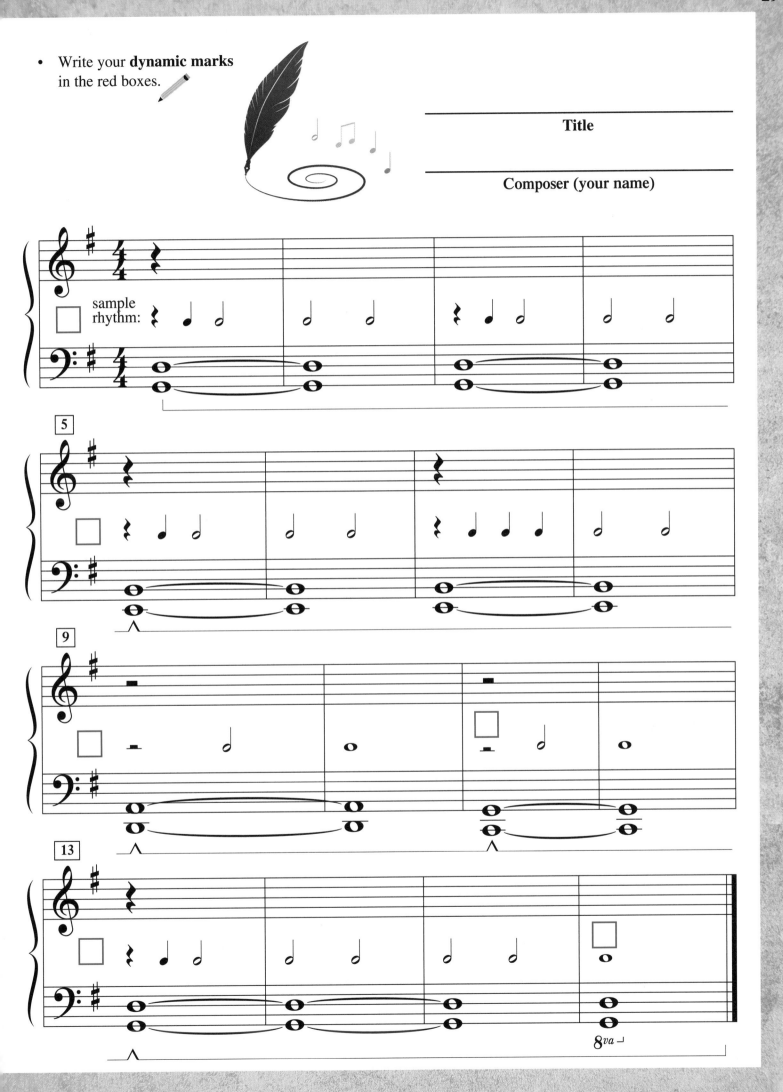

- Write your **dynamic marks** in the red boxes.

Title

Composer (your name)

DICTIONARY PUZZLE

Use terms from the **Music Dictionary** (p. 32)
to complete the puzzle.

ACROSS

2. Abbreviation for *mezzo-forte*.

4. Play gradually louder.

7. A curved line that tells us to play *legato*.

8. *mp* Moderately soft.

9. Depress the damper pedal.

10. Play detached, disconnected.

11. Abbreviation for *mezzo piano*.

12. *f* Loud.

16. Play connected.

17. Hold this note its full value.

19. Play gradually softer.

20. Resume the original tempo.

21. Play this note louder.

22. Hold this note longer than usual.

23. Fast, lively tempo.

DOWN

1. $\frac{4}{4}$ Indicates how many beats in a measure and what note gets the beat.

3. *mf*   Moderately loud.

5. ♪   An ornamental note played quickly into the note that follows.

6.   Rather fast, but not as fast as allegro.

9. *p*   Soft.

11.   Moderately.

13. *8va*   Play one octave higher (or lower) than written.

14. *rit.*   Gradually slow down.

15.   Gradually play faster.

18.   A main melody of a piece.

MUSIC DICTIONARY

pp	*p*	*mp*	*mf*	*f*
pianissimo	*piano*	*mezzo-piano*	*mezzo-forte*	*forte*
very soft	soft	medium soft	medium loud	loud

crescendo (cresc.)
Play gradually louder.

diminuendo (dim.) or **decrescendo (decresc.)**
Play gradually softer.

SIGN	TERM	DEFINITION
♪ (accent)	**accent**	Play this note louder.
accel.	*accelerando*	Gradually play faster.
	Alberti bass	A broken chord accompaniment that uses the pattern: bottom-top-middle-top
	allegretto	Rather fast, but not as fast as *allegro*.
	allegro	Fast, lively tempo.
	a tempo	Resume original tempo (speed).
𝄐	*fermata*	Hold this note longer than usual.
♪ (grace note)	**grace note**	An ornamental note that is played quickly into the note that follows.
	half step	Two keys immediately next to each other with no note in between. (C-C♯ or E-F)
	legato	Play smoothly, connected.
	moderato	Medium speed.
8va – ¬	*ottava*	Play one octave higher than written. When 8va – ⌐ is below the staff, play one octave lower.
⌞__⌟	**pedal mark**	Depress the damper (right-foot pedal) after you play the note or chord; release at the end of the pedal mark.
___∧___	**pedal change**	Lift the pedal on the beat and depress immediately after.
	pentatonic scale	A 5-note scale popular in Chinese music.
rit.	*ritard*	Gradually slow down. Short for *ritardando*.
(slur)	**slur**	Shows a musical phrase. Connect the notes.
♪ (staccato)	*staccato*	Play notes marked *staccato* detached, disconnected.
♪ (tenuto)	**tenuto**	Hold this note its full value. Hint: Press deeply into the key.
	theme	The main melody of a piece.
	trill	A rapid alternation of two keys next to each other.